The Big Bike Ride

By Ilana Stack

Library For All Ltd.

LIBRARY FOR ALL
DIGITAL EDUCATION · FOR THE WORLD

Library For All is an Australian not for profit organisation with a mission to make knowledge accessible to all via an innovative digital library solution. Visit us at libraryforall.org

The Big Bike Ride

First published 2023

Published by Library For All Ltd
Email: info@libraryforall.org
URL: libraryforall.org

Our Yarning logo design by Jason Lee, Bidjipidji Art

Original illustrations by Hannah Bryce

The Big Bike Ride
Stack, Ilana
ISBN: 978-1-922991-11-9
SKU01319

The Big Bike Ride

We respect and honour Aboriginal and Torres Strait Islander Elders past, present and future. We acknowledge the stories, traditions and living cultures of Aboriginal and Torres Strait Islander peoples on this land and commit to building a brighter future together.

It's a lovely, sunny day and Lindsay and his nan are going on a big bike ride along the Swan River.

What will they see?

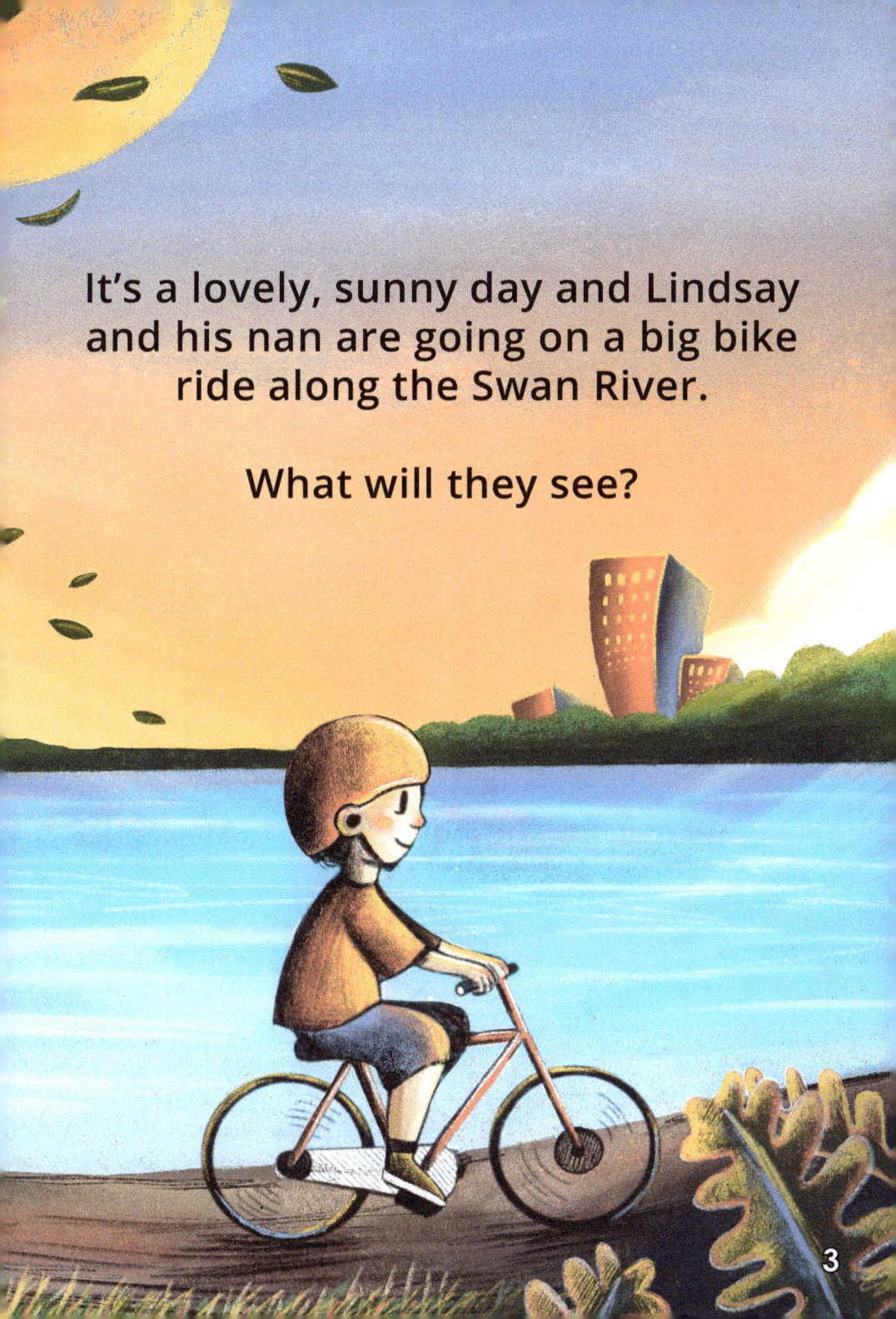

They saw some boats, ducks, swans and dogs playing.

There were people fishing, and people walking and riding their bikes on the path with them.

4

Lindsay rode across a large
bridge and saw some big birds
on the water.

Pelicans!

Lindsay was very excited when he saw them and called out, "Hello, Mr Pelican!"

Flap, flap, went the
big wings as they flew
away across the river.

"Bye, Mr Pelican!"

Back on their bikes, Nan said,
"OH NO! My bike has a flat tyre!
We need to fix it so we can
get home!"

Nan and Lindsay took the bikes under a shady tree and Nan got her bike kit out.

"Lindsay, can you hold the bike for me please?" asked Nan.

"Yes! I can help you, Nan,"
said Lindsay.

Nan patched the tyre and got
the pump out. Lindsay wanted
to help pump air into the tyres.

He pumped and pumped until his arms got sore and then he asked Nan to help him.

Nan and Lindsay got the tyre
fixed and rode to the shop for
an ice-cream.

They went and sat near the
river to watch all the fun.

Lick, lick! Yum, yum!

What fun they had on their
big bike ride.

You can use these questions to talk about this book with your family, friends and teachers.

What did you learn from this book?

Describe this book in one word. Funny? Scary? Colourful? Interesting?

How did this book make you feel when you finished reading it?

What was your favourite part of this book?

download our reader app
getlibraryforall.org

About the author

Ilana was born in Perth and is from the Noongar, Yamajti and Nyariyin Nations of WA. She loves taking her grandsons to the park to play and telling them stories, their favourite is *The Story of the Three Little Pigs*.

Our Yarning

Want to discover more books from this collection? Our Yarning is a collection of books written by Aboriginal and Torres Strait Islander peoples across Australia.

We know that children learn better, and enjoy reading more, when they see themselves in the stories, characters and illustrations of the books they read.

To download the app, visit the Google Play Store on any Android device and search 'Our Yarning'.

libraryforall.org

www.ingramcontent.com/pod-product-compliance
Lightning Source LLC
Chambersburg PA
CBHW040122070426
42448CB00042B/3408